THE PICTURE LIFE OF DWIGHT GOODEN

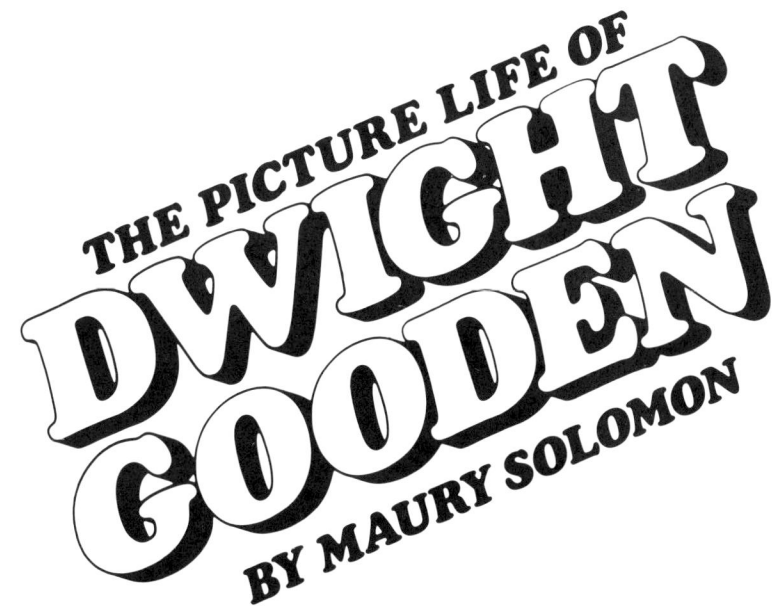

THE PICTURE LIFE OF DWIGHT GOODEN
BY MAURY SOLOMON

FRANKLIN WATTS
NEW YORK LONDON TORONTO
SYDNEY 1986

R. L. 3.4 Spache Revised Formula

Cover photograph courtesy
of Tony Triolo/*Sports Illustrated*

Photographs courtesy of:
Ronald Madra/*Sports Illustrated*: pp. 6, 25, 26;
AP/Wide World Photos: pp. 9, 21, 27, 31, 32, 35, 43;
Manny Rubio/*Sports Illustrated*: pp. 10, 13, 17;
UPI/Bettmann Newsphotos: pp. 14, 18, 22, 28, 40;
Tony Triolo/*Sports Illustrated*: p. 36;
Manny Millan/*Sports Illustrated*: p. 39;
Walter Iooss, Jr./*Sports Illustrated*: p. 44.

Library of Congress Cataloging in Publication Data

Solomon, Maury.
The picture life of Dwight Gooden.

Includes index.
Summary: A brief biography emphasizing the career of
the Mets pitcher who won the 1985 National League
Cy Young Award by unanimous vote.
1. Gooden, Dwight—Juvenile literature. 2. Baseball
players—United States—Biography—Juvenile literature.
[1. Gooden, Dwight. 2. Baseball players. 3. Afro-
Americans—Biography] I. Title.
GV865.G62S65 1986 796.357'092'4 [B] [92] 86-1636
IBSN 0-531-10193-2

Copyright © 1986 by Maury Solomon
All rights reserved
Printed in the United States of America
6 5 4 3 2 1

IN MEMORY OF MY FATHER,
WITH WHOM I SHARED
THE AGONIES AND THE ECSTASIES
OF THE EARLY METS

It was a heartbreaking ending for Mets players and fans. 1985 was to be the year the Mets would return to glory. The team had the talent. They had the dreams and wishes of fans who remembered 1969. That was the year the Mets had won it all. And they had their young right-handed pitching star, Dwight Gooden.

But they finished second in the Eastern Division. Just one day before the regular season ended, the Mets were eliminated from an exciting division race. The St. Louis Cardinals beat them and went on to win the National League championship. The Cardinals were later defeated in the World Series by the Kansas City Royals.

There was nothing second place about Dwight Gooden, however. Gooden, in only his second year in the big leagues, dazzled the baseball world with his achievements. A mere twenty years old, Gooden won 24 games and lost only 4. This was the best record in baseball that year. He ended the 1985 season with an ERA of 1.53, the

Gooden is congratulated by third baseman Howard Johnson after beating the St. Louis Cardinals 5-2 for Gooden's 24th win of the 1985 season.

lowest in both leagues. (ERA stands for "earned runned average." It refers to how many runs per game a pitcher allows.) He struck out 268 batters and gave up only 198 hits in 277 innings pitched. He walked only 69 batters in the entire season. In fact, his walk-to-hit ratio was one of the best in history. Many think that Dwight Gooden has the potential to become the best pitcher in the history of modern baseball.

Dwight was born on November 16, 1964, in East Tampa, Florida. His father was a chemical-plant worker. His mother was a nurse's aide. He was the youngest member of his family. This included three

Dwight with his proud parents
at their home in Florida

older brothers, James, Danny, and Charles, who were from his father's first marriage. They did not live with Dwight. Dwight also had two older sisters, Mercedes and Betty.

When he was six years old, Dwight's father took him to see the Detroit Tigers in spring training. He saw Al Kaline hit, and from that point on he wanted to be a baseball player and hit home runs. His father had played and coached semipro ball in Florida. So he encouraged his son. At seven Dwight joined the Belmar Heights Little League as a pitcher. But he was shy and quit the team. Over the next few years, he joined and quit teams several times.

Father and son—both lifelong baseball fans

By ten, though, Dwight was back playing baseball to stay. He switched from pitching to playing third base. At twelve he returned to pitching and pitched a perfect game.

Dwight had some problems with his temper when he was a youngster. He hated to lose and got angry at other players who were not as talented as he was. But eventually he learned to control his temper. In fact, one of the things he is most admired for today is his poise and coolness under pressure. He says in his autobiography, *Rookie*, published by Doubleday in 1985, "If things start going wrong for you, you've got to ask yourself: Why do something stupid? Why get mad? Forget about it. Blank it out of your mind and get the next hitter."

Pitching in one of his first major league games, young Gooden displays the poise of an old pro.

Gooden went to Hillsborough High School in Tampa. His baseball coach there was Billy Reed. Gooden recalls that "Reed was a tough coach, probably the toughest I've had. He got everything out of you he could, forced you to use all your talent."

It was in high school that Dwight got the nickname Doc. He idolized Julius Erving, a basketball player whose nickname was Dr. J. Dwight had a good fastball and struck out a lot of batters. When friends saw he had his fastball going, they'd yell out to him, "Operate on him, Doc!" "K" is an abbreviation for strikeout. Dwight's fans often call him "Dr. K" because of his strikeout record.

Dwight (middle row, far left) and school teammates take the field again at a high-school reunion.

Gooden thought about going to college. But he wasn't a great student. And he really wanted to play professional baseball. He decided that if he wasn't drafted by the big leagues, he would go to the University of Miami. (The draft gives all professional clubs, especially losing ones, a chance to sign up talented young players their scouts have discovered.)

In the June draft of 1982, Gooden was chosen by the New York Mets. He was the fifth pick on the first round. He was astounded. He thought he might be drafted, but not on the first round. "I never kept up with the Mets, didn't even know they had spring training in St. Pete. I was never even talked to by a scout of the Mets, as far as I can remember."

Mets scouts spotted Gooden's rare talent early on.

But the Mets organization knew him. Getting Dwight to sign up with the Mets was part of Nelson Doubleday's plan. Nelson Doubleday, Jr., is the owner of the Mets. He had bought the club in 1980. (He also owns a large publishing company bearing his name.)

Doubleday wanted to build a pennant-contending team from young, talented players developed by the Mets own farm (Minor League) system. Darryl Strawberry, the 1983 Rookie of the Year, was another such player signed by Doubleday.

Gooden reported to Kingsport, Tennessee, to the Appalachian League for Rookie Ball on June 15, 1982. His salary was $600 a month, which is the same for all rookies, plus an $85,000 bonus.

Nelson Doubleday, owner of the Mets, knows how to pick his rookies.

This was the first time Dwight had been away from home. In his autobiography he says, "Besides getting pitching experience, the main thing I was learning in the Rookie League was how to manage being away from your home and family and being on your own."

In 1983, he played in the South Atlantic League at Lynchburg. He finished the 1983 season with a 19–4 record. He also set a league record of 300 strikeouts.

After 1984 spring training, Dwight thought he would be going to the Mets' Minor League club at Tidewater when the Mets traveled north. But the Mets lost their veteran pitcher Tom Seaver to the White Sox and needed another starter. Davey Johnson, the Met manager, decided that his new starter would be Number 16, Dwight Gooden.

Gooden in action in an early 1984 game.

Dwight's rookie year in the big leagues rocked the baseball world. He struck out more batters (276) than any other rookie pitcher in history, toppling Herb Score's record of thirty years' standing. Young fans at Shea Stadium in New York started putting up big red "K" signs in the outfield to keep track of Gooden's strikeout total. Thus was born the "K Korner." (Fans in other cities often set up their own "K Korners" when Dwight pitches there.)

With each strike-out, fans hang another K in the K Korner in Shea Stadium's upper decks.

The stands are a sea of K's when the Doctor is on the mound. Opposite: the "krowded" K Korner at the San Francisco Giants' stadium in Candlestick Park.

Gooden set many other records that season. He came in second in the league in ERA, with 2.60. He was the youngest player ever to play in an All-Star game, where he struck out three batters in a row after Dodger pitcher Fernando Valenzuela had just struck out three. This set a new All-Star record for the most strikeouts in a row. Dwight won the 1984 Rookie of the Year Award. He was the youngest ever to be Rookie of the Year. He also came in second (to Rick Sutcliffe) in the balloting for the Cy Young Award. The Cy Young Award is the top award any pitcher can win. It is voted upon each year by twenty-four members of the Baseball Writers Association of America.

Pitching in the All-Star Game
on July 10, 1984, in San Francisco

Dwight's major problem in 1984 concerned men on base. Runners stole many bases off of him. He worked hard over the winter to adjust his pitching style to keep runners close. And he worked on his pickoff move, hoping to throw out runners on first base who were "napping."

Gooden got a large raise for the next season. He would be making $325,000 in salary. Plus, he would receive $150,000 in bonuses—if he performed as well as he had in his rookie year.

Dwight takes a "Gooden" look at first base before delivering the pitch. In 1985 he was much better at holding runners close —and picking off those who strayed too far.

He didn't do as well. He did better. Much better. In addition to all the achievements mentioned earlier, Gooden became the youngest pitcher ever to win twenty games. He won fourteen in a row, setting a new club record. He became the youngest pitcher ever to win the Cy Young Award. He was even considered for the MVP (Most Valuable Player) award, though he didn't win it. Pitchers are rarely ever considered for this award. This is because many feel that it should go to an everyday player, since there is the Cy Young Award for pitching.

Many compare Gooden to Houston pitching great Nolan Ryan, one of Gooden's childhood idols. Gooden has a blazing

Dwight shows his winning form, defeating the San Diego Padres 9-3 and becoming the youngest 20-game winner in Major League history on August 25, 1985.

fastball, clocked at around 95 miles an hour. He also has a dazzling curveball that "bends like elbow macaroni," in the words of one sports reporter. And he has a good changeup. Gooden says he eventually wants to develop a slider, too. But the Mets don't want him to work on that too much now. Sliders require an extra twist of the arm. The Mets are afraid he will hurt his young arm with the slider.

Despite his Florida upbringing, Dwight doesn't like pitching in very hot weather. He wears long sleeves throughout the season. He stands 6 feet 3 inches tall and weighs around 195 pounds. His classic high kick and smooth follow-through are beautiful to watch.

Gooden finished the 1985 season with the year's best record: 24-4. A Mets clubhouse joke at the time: If only Dwight hadn't lost those 4 games, the Mets would have gone to the Series.

Gooden is an all-round athlete and is a very good hitter for a pitcher. He enjoys batting more than most other pitchers. He originally wanted to play third base or the outfield. This would have allowed him to play every day and bat more often. His first Major League hit was against Fernando Valenzuela in May of his first year. In his 22nd win of the 1985 season, he got three hits, including his first home run. He told reporters after that game that he'd trade a home run for a no-hitter any day (though his fans certainly wouldn't!). One reporter asked him how often he really thought about hitting home runs. He said, "Just about every time I come to the plate."

Dwight is one pitcher who loves to hit.

Gooden's closest friend on the team is Darryl Strawberry. Strawberry won the Rookie of the Year Award the year before Gooden did. Gooden also says that teammates George Foster and Keith Hernandez were very steadying influences on him his first year. Working with Gary Carter behind the plate in 1985 was another dream come true for Gooden. He had admired Carter for years.

Dwight keeps in close touch with his family during the season. He calls his parents after each game he pitches. He has bought his family a new house and lives with them in the off-season.

Gary Carter congratulates the Doc on another win.

Dwight likes rock music and jazz. He also likes watching the soap operas on TV. He loves basketball and used to play it. But he avoids playing it now for fear of injury.

Though he recently became engaged to Carlene Pearson, Dwight says they do not plan to marry right away. Dwight wants to concentrate all his energies on baseball for a little while longer. His goal now is to play in a World Series. He says, "Baseball has been everything to me for about as long as I can remember. That's all I've dreamed, eaten, slept. I could go out and play ball every day, year round, if I had somebody to play with."

The 1985 National League Cy Young Award winner and birthday boy receives hugs from his sister Betty Gooden Jones (left) and his fiancee Carlene Pearson.

Gooden's 1985 season compares well with baseball's greatest pitchers. This includes Grover Cleveland Alexander, Warren Spahn, Bob Gibson, and Sandy Koufax—during their greatest seasons. Some of these pitchers won more games per season or had a better fastball. But none had as good an overall record so young or such an outstanding walk-to-hit ratio. The walk-to-hit ratio is considered one of the best ways to determine a pitcher's overall effectiveness.

Much of Dwight's success is due to his much talked-about "control." He has it both on the field and when talking to the press. He doesn't enjoy talking to the press, because he's still basically a quiet and shy person. But he knows it is part of his job and can help him, the club, and baseball.

Signing autographs
for fans at Shea

In February 1986, Dwight signed a new contract with the Mets. He will get $1.32 million for the 1986 season, making him one of the highest paid players in baseball today.

All the attention Dwight has gotten has not changed him. He is liked by his teammates and admired by fans all over the country. And parents of young fans appreciate Dwight's strong sense of values, devotion to his family, and clean living. They think he sets a good example for children.

Though he is certainly a "strikeout" pitcher, Dwight is most concerned with winning and with doing his job well. He hates to let people down and he still hates to lose.

It is a safe bet to say that there won't be much losing in the future of this young, talented athlete. All baseball fans will share in the excitement that will surely come from watching Dwight Gooden in action in the years ahead.

FAST FACT SHEETS

1984 SEASON

Won-Lost Record: 17-9
Innings Pitched: 218
ERA: 2.60
Hits Allowed: 161
Base on Balls: 73
Strikeouts: 276

- 1984 National League Rookie of the Year.
- Led the Major Leagues with 276 strikeouts, breaking the rookie record.
- Established a Major League record with an average of 11.39 strikeouts per nine innings.

- Broke a National League record with 32 strikeouts in two consecutive games; set a Major League record with 43 strikeouts in three consecutive games.
- Established club records with fifteen 10-plus strikeout games and five consecutive 10-plus strikeout games.
- Was the youngest player ever to play in an All-Star game.

1985 SEASON

Won-Lost Record: 24-4
Innings Pitched: 277
ERA: 1.53
Hits Allowed: 198
Base on Balls: 69
Strikeouts: 268

- Won the 1985 National League Cy Young Award by a unanimous vote. (This has happened only seven times in the 29-year history of the award.) Was the youngest player ever to win this award.

- Won the "Triple Crown" of pitching by leading both leagues in wins, strikeouts, and lowest ERA. (Became only the seventh player in history to do so and the first player to do it since Sandy Koufax of the L.A. Dodgers in 1966.)
- Was the youngest Major League pitcher ever to start an opening day game and to win 20 games in a season.
- Out of 35 starts, pitched 16 complete games and 8 shutouts, giving up only 13 home runs and 47 earned runs all year.